Find Your Tribe.

By Mike Stallard.

For the stale, for the beginner and,
above all, for the man in the pew
who you serve. I hope this will
give you some fresh ideas to
inspire you.

- Mike Stallard

TABLE OF CONTENTS

I very much hope that this booklet
will give you a lot of fresh ideas..

I have taken great care

WHAT IS THE POINT OF THIS LITTLE BOOK?

The author was himself once a preacher in a Church in Norfolk where he was the Rector. So he knows the pitfalls only too well. They still make him go hot and cold when he reviews his mistakes. Since his conversion to Catholicism some 30 years ago, he has been a layman. Over his life, he has sat in the pews in several different countries – Singapore, Australia, Morocco, France, Spain – and listened as much as he could.

This booklet contains his hints to preachers on how to get through to the people sitting next to him at the back of the church.

TALKING ABOUT GOD THE HOLY TRINITY.

Think of the boy who has been brought kicking and screaming, without his Dad, to Church. He has to sit through your talk.

Think of the people out there who are not in the tribe. Strict tribal rules have been broken. They might be divorced. They might have lost their faith. They might not have been to confession before the Mass.

You have to explain – not just quote – the Bible.

You have to bring out the meaning of the life of Christ.

You have to think through the minds of the people who are paying you the courtesy of listening to you.

I have sat through all sorts of services in the last 30 years at the back of the church. I have seen the squirming adolescent, the puzzled man dying of cancer, the weeping widow, the desperate divorcee with her two boys, the immigrant struggling with a new language. Rarely have I seen the priest connect with such people.

Rarely – but I have certainly seen it happen.

A friend told me that she went to an open confession and, after a lot of prayer and thought, confessed that she had not been coming to church because she was a divorcée. The priest surprised her by throwing his arms round her neck and embracing her! "Welcome home!" He said. She has come to church ever since, although the priest himself died some years ago now.

It is all still there. We have to describe it for the blind so that they see.

MY TRIBE.

Everybody is in a tribe of some sort or another.

For example, my own father was in the Conservative Tribe. He was also in the Church of England Tribe where he was a Vicar. He was in the FEPO tribe – the Far Eastern Prisoners of War tribe because he had been taken prisoner at Singapore. He was also in the male tribe because of his sexuality. My Mum was in other tribes. The Mothers Union. The female tribe. The family tribe.

Nothing wrong in any of that.

So long as you yourself do not have to join!

You have your own tribe too.

For instance, the Labour tribe. You want everyone to work together for the good of everyone else and are horrified – or pretend to be horrified – when they don't. Or the Conservative tribe which is the party of government and which has its own rules and customs too. The Prime Minister was in the Bullingdon Tribe with its own strange rules of how to behave. I know of a very important man who supports the Tottenham Hotspur tribe.

But you get the point.

We Christians are another tribe, or rather a set of tribes. We are exclusive. *You* have to join *us*. *You* have to obey *our* rules. Inside our tribe, *you* can get promotion within the tribe and perhaps become a chief. You can gain respect from other tribal members. And, of course, we ourselves have several different sub tribes too. And quite often there are tribal wars and disputes about tribal behaviour.

My father in law, after a distinguished career as a bomber pilot and headmaster, upbraided me when I became a Catholic, left my parish, where I had been a Rector, and went

9/86

on the dole. "If I had been there I would have been a Bishop!"
For him, the Church was just another ladder to climb.

You have to join up. And, from the outside, frankly, *we* aren't
very attractive. Ancient people. Ancient buildings, silly,
ancient clothes which aren't really ancient. Silly voices for
boring services. We also have special disapproving faces and
we say extremely silly and out of date things which have long
ago been disproved by science. Oh - and we are smug.

Your job, as a preacher, is to sell our tribe. But also, of course,
it is to reinforce our own tribal loyalties too.

How?

Here are some suggestions:

OUR OWN TOOL KIT.

We have the Bible. We have today's readings. We have our own rules. We have our own traditions. And all these things need to be interpreted, explained, reinforced from year to year, from week to week.

I am surprised how, when the plague locks us all up in the spring of 2020, how tribal we become. Defensively all the churches are locked tight shut. In Abu Dhabi, the call to prayer still rings out five times a day from the deserted Mosque.

Our local priest has gone online and provided a survival kit for his parish. It consists of the rosary, exposition of the blessed sacrament and a Facebook site. The Archbishop of Canterbury gives us his thoughts in words. Nothing wrong with any of that. The faithful need to be looked after.

But the challenge all the time is balancing welcome with tribalism. The closer knit the tribe, the more unwritten and written rules there are, the closer the tribe knits together, the more cliquey it becomes. Exclusive. Joining it takes more and more determination. On the other hand, wishy-washy beliefs which demand nothing are just as repellent. If you believe in nothing much, then what have you got to offer?

Far too many protestant churches demand nothing. So that is what they get back. Methodist Chapels round here – and there are plenty of them – have either been converted into garages or pulled down. The preacher's path has been built over. Ministers are very few and far between. Their political arm – the Labour movement – has now lost much of its religious input. Ask nothing and – get nothing.

Let us remember that Muslims – our brother religion – are told to pray five times a day and to eat and drink nothing in the desert heat between dawn and dusks. And that is just for starters...

So how tribal are you going to be?

How many rules are you going to insist on?

How many tribal customs and traditions will you support?

At one end of the spectrum you have the exclusive clique, which can well lead to the defensive violence of despair as the foundations start to crumble, and at the other end you have the gaping nothing of nihilism, modern art and Nietzsche. Have you not heard, said the clown? "God is dead".

Here are some ideas which may help:

WHY PREACH AT ALL?

Let us listen to a Muslim. I like Muslims! I really do. I used to fear them. Now I can see that they really are our brothers in the fight.

But that does not mean that they are always right: they are not.

Ibn Khaldun wrote a long, difficult book called *the Muqaddimah* (Footsteps) in the year of the hegira 750 or thereabouts, towards the end of our Middle Ages. His brilliant mind listed seven reasons to speak in public.

Here they are:

1. You want to promote a new branch of knowledge.

2. You want to open a difficult work to other people.

3. You want to discuss an error in a learned book.

4. You want to fill out a discipline (or a part of the liturgy?)

5. You want to edit a book and put it into order.

6. You want to make a collection of works on a subject which interests you.

7. You want to condense a book which has too much verbiage.

To many people the Bible is a completely unopened book. It needs explaining.

- When,

- where,

- what happened,

- how it happened

- who was involved,

- why is it important today?

You need to know the answers to all these six journalist's questions. And that goes for the Bible readings which you have just listened to. How rarely do we in the pews hear them discussed in this way! That simply?

And you need to explain them that simply and using simple words. The mark of an alpha mind is to make the very difficult seem simple.

And yes, the bible has its errors. Do not be afraid to talk about them.

There are mistakes in the text for a start.

The writer, tired and with aching wrists, looks away and writes the wrong word. He reads something which must be wrong, so he corrects it. Don't forget that he cannot rub out indelible ink from an expensive page. Maybe he writes the same word twice or leaves out a crucial word. Then he just goes on, perhaps not even noticing, perhaps hoping that nobody will notice if he distracts the eye with a golden picture or some nice curly squiggles.

And the writers were all men of their time, gliding the soft pen across the expensive paper. They assumed things. For ibn Khaldun, the world was a dome rising from surrounding waters. Above him, the planets, the stars, the sun, circled mysteriously as if in a bowl. Nothing wrong with that in the days before the telescope. As far as I can make out, the psalmists thought the same thing.

The Bible is inspired by God, yes. But written by fallible men.

And lots of rules! The ten commandments are just one example. What does just one of them imply for us today? The golden rule: how can you love you neighbour if you have not even got a clue what their name is? How do you serve the

Lord, your God with all your mind, soul, heart and strength in today's godless society?

Lets' stop pretending that the Bible was written by idiots too. St John's Gospel: the word for charcoal (anthrakia) appears just twice. Once round the *charcoal* fire when Peter strongly denies that he has ever had anything to do with Jesus; twice when Jesus, (and this is after his death!), produces fish and a *charcoal* fire and Peter and the others sit round it. Then Jesus warmly forgives him. Did you know that? The writer of this Gospel had a surprisingly sharp eye for detail.

The two millennia have given us Christians a lot of time linking passages intertwined in both old and new testaments. Going back and looking at the linking texts is useful too. "A virgin shall conceive and bear a son." "My God, my God, why have you forsaken me?"

Let's just take one example of teasing out the New Testament from the Old: Jesus is "Son of David". King David. We are talking about a man who could not suppress his lust for a naked woman, his gay love of Jonathan, his small sins like eating the sacred bread, and his very big sins too like numbering the people (what is that all about?). A man of magnificent generosity, a man who could weep, dance almost naked in public, a slayer of wild beasts – and Goliath! A generous man who could spare the life of a mad king who was out to exterminate him.

Don't be afraid to condense the Bible or other great pieces of Christian literature. Better condensed than left out.

Talk about God the Father. Talk about God the Son. Talk about the Holy Spirit. Go on – that is what people come to church for.

You have my full permission!

Once, when I was still a Rector, I had to take a service in a prison. The week after I did that, the Catholic Priest was taken hostage by the inmates and held for several hours.

I took some incense and asked for a volunteer to swing the censer. Derisively, the men selected a reject. He came shyly up and we lit the charcoal together. Then, through the service, he swung the censor with pride.

I hadn't prepared for the service, I must admit. It was only matins after all.

So after the readings, as so often when I had not prepared anything, I felt obliged to speak. I told them that Jesus was a much harder criminal than they were. None of them had been executed or scourged. None of them had been through two trials with false witnesses and not even opened their mouths. I doubted if any of them had been spat at by the police either.

And they listened. At the end, the censer was handed back to me and they trooped out. Isn't there something in the Gospels about not worrying about what you are going to say because it will be given to you on the spot?

Result? I haven't got a clue. But God has.

So how do you start?

If you feel like it, start with a prayer or Bible quote: "In the name of the Father, and of the Son and of the Holy Spirit." Or you can be clever and find one for yourself. The beginning and end of St Paul's epistles are a good place to look.

Now what?

Most preachers have a favourite start. Every single week they depend on it until it begins to grate. Politicians are even worse...

Here are six totally different ways – fresh ways – to start your talk. Look through, choose your start and go for it!

- *Be nice.*

After leaving the Church of England, I worked for three months at Olan Mills, selling glamour photos. I was trained by their top sales team. I went to Middlesborough and was put up in a hotel. I went to the local office to be greeted by a tall, slender lady in a more or less transparent linen dress. Well groomed, charming, helpful, nice. She taught me how to sell. And her first lesson was that it is the person who sells the product.

I then went to Leicester to practise what she had taught me. I went as an art expert complete with my balding head and little spectacles. The first sale was a disaster. I held back. I told a few jokes. At the end the head of the (Indian) family politely asked me how old I thought they were. He then carefully explained that they did not like to be condescended to and left without a sale. In came the manager. She shouted at me that I had better get selling properly or else I would be dismissed that day. I listened contritely and did exactly what the lady at Middlesborough had told me to do word for word.

Bingo!

Niceness is not weakness; niceness is not holding back. It is politely going for it!

After that I went back to Leeds and our team soon became the very best in the whole company. We had a superb photographer, an excellent make over expert and a friendly receptionist. So selling their products was simple. We were nice and our product was nice. People began telling their friends about how nice we were. We went viral...

* *Help the reader/audience with some timely advice.*

20/86

What a horrible rainy Sunday morning! - Whew! That was a long Gospel, was it not? - Let's get stuck into this extraordinary story. - It's really hot in here could someone please open a window or two? - It's cold because the boiler is on the blink. It will be sorted by next Sunday though. It is nice listening to stuff like that. It shows the preacher is listening's

- *Explain succinctly what you are going to say.*

Sometimes a Bible story or a part of the service needs teasing out. Retell the story simply, along with the background and the journalist's questions (When, where, what, who, how, why?). Go for it! Don't waste our time back here in the pews with some silly story or a feeble joke – or three. Just get on with it. And finish with why it has anything to do with me living, as I do, two millennia after it was written in the first place.

- *Start with a story.*

It could be a story out of the Bible. In a talk about brotherly love, for instance, it might be good to start with Cain who was killed by his brother Abel. Or perhaps when Jacob swindled Esau out of his inheritance by a dastardly trick. (It all came home when Laban, his employer, swindled him even more cruelly.) How about something on the love that Judah showed his younger brother Joseph by abandoning him in the desert to die?

One of the memorable talks I have listened to was in Spain. In Spanish. I couldn't understand much of it. But the chorus of each paragraph I have never forgotten "Yak pasado". It means: *That's history*. If it is a piece of your own personal (boring) history, then keep it short and *always* link it to what you are trying to say. As I am trying to do.

A missionary priest told us how he had had a gun held at his head in Nigeria. He had then been ordered to accompany the gunman on a walk from which the priest knew he would never return. The priest knelt down, he told us, and prayed. This is what he prayed: "Forgive me my sins. Thank you for everything. See you in a minute." He went on to tell us that the gunman had second thoughts and left without killing him. We were left to draw our own conclusions.

So how does that story influence this paragraph? Well, I think it shows that starting off with a story, and this is a good one, gets people's attention. And it also shows that it has nothing to do with what I am trying to get across to you, the reader. Shame! It is a good story.

- *Explain exactly what the opposition are on about.*

Now is your chance to attack the media, the BBC, ITV, sexism, the internet, feminism, XR, peanut butter manufacturers and, of course, the government! Six feet above criticism too!

Sometimes, yes, we Christians just have to state our case. Just be careful, that's all. There will be media people, BBC listeners, ITV lovers, sexists, lovers of peanut butter, geeks, etc etc in your congregation and you will have to face them in just a few minutes...

- *Tell a joke.*

Usually an old, well-worn one. Tired old one. Favourite old one. And, do you know what? I have listened to probably a thousand sermons and homilies in my life and I cannot remember a single joke that made me laugh. No, not one. But of all the ways of starting off this is the most common.

Why?

Here's the underlying thinking:

I want to come over as a nice person. But, if you
aren't careful, you see, people are offended. So I
won't make them laugh too much and I'll avoid all
difficult topics too. You don't want that do you.
Especially in Church...

Weak, weak, weak...

- *What do the audience want from you? Meet their
  need.*

Feel for your listeners. What are they yearning for? What are
they there for? How can you help get them there? Are they
there for reassurance? Are they there because they have
been told to be there? Have they some awful secret to hide?
This can well be linked to a story either from your own life, or
perhaps from the Bible or some other book. I often use the
Tao as devotional reading. Not very Christian, but the Tao
proclaims the mystery and power of God in a very special
Chinese way and I like that.

This set of ideas is written for you experienced preachers as
well. We all have our favourite turn of phrase, our own little
tricks. And as the years go by, we get stuck in a rut. After that

it is same old same old. People feel they have heard it all before.

As an ex-preacher and as someone who has then spent 30 years in the pew listening, I want to pull rank here!

If you try a few new ways to start, you can get off to a new, fresh start. Like wearing a crisp new jacket.

Like starting all over again.

OK Now you've got that start sorted, what next?

Is this what you were expecting?

7 Steps to a Good Sermon or How to Create and Preach a Sermon

1. ***Get a Text to Preach*** – There are many ways to get a text. The preacher can choose a text. The preacher can use a lectionary like the Revised Common Lectionary that assigns a text. The preacher can create a sermonic plan that incorporates and includes a list of texts. One preacher told me that he daily reads the Bible devotionally and then he writes down insights. When it is time to preach he goes through his notes for the previous year to find themes and texts to preach.

2. ***Interpret the Text For Preaching*** – Biblical exegesis consists of reading the text closely. An outline method that I use for exegesis is from Dr. Brad Braxton. He looks at the text from a few angles to get a well rounded view of the text. First he gets his initial impressions of the text by reading it in various translations and noting whatever comes to his mind in relation to the text. Then he goes to a literary analysis where he carefully examines the literary structure of the text. Here we look at exactly what is said in the text. Then he does an analysis of the Historical and

Rhetorical dimensions of the text under consideration. Here we look at the history behind the text including the author and the hearers of the text. Finally, Dr. Braxton looks at the Theological and Contextual dimensions of the text. Here we seek to understand the social context of the text and the theology of the writers and hearers of the text.

You can see his process more fully in the book <u>Preaching Paul</u>.

3. ***Get a Theme for the Sermon*** – What is the point of your sermon? Here you look at your exegesis and determine what does God want the hearers to get from the sermon and how do you think the hearers should respond to the sermon? In other words what does the Sermon Claim about the Gospel and what do you want the people to do as a result of hearing the sermon.

4. ***Write the Sermon*** – Using the theme of the sermon and the exegesis, write the sermon. Be sure to structure your sermon in a way that makes sense. By that I mean that the movement of the sermon makes sense and would not be confusing to the hearers. I try to write my first draft as quickly as possible.

5. ***Prepare Sermon for Preaching (Editing and Polishing)*** – If you have written your sermon very quickly then it is time to actually edit the sermon. Condense the sermon by getting rid of words that are redundant. You also want to get rid of theological concepts that might be hard to understand for the hearers. You don't have to dumb down the content, but you must state whatever you have to say in a clear way.

6. ***Practice the Sermon*** – Go over the sermon in your mind or out loud. Reading the sermon out loud will help you to

continue the editing. You will find some parts don't make
sense and other parts can be made more clear. You will
also gain a greater command of your sermon.

7. ***Preach the Sermon With Confidence*** – Go ahead and
present the sermon. You have prepared, you have a Biblical
sermon because you did adequate exegesis. You have an
interesting and informative sermon because you came up
with the sermonic point and you have an idea of how the
people should respond to the sermon.

Someone asked once how long should each step take? Well that
is a hard question, it should take as long as it takes you to finish
the point. But I do wish to add that you will never be totally
finished in sermon preparation even after the presentation of the
sermon. So you must prepare enough…what that means
depends on who you are…

(Courtesy to this site, *soul preaching*, which I got off the net.)

This is sincere – definitely. But with disadvantages.
I have sat through a lot of sermons like this. I am
afraid they are usually terribly boring. The life went
out of them shortly between the second and third
stages. And they often come over as completely
false too.

I am afraid that I have even had to sit through
several sermons which were written by someone

else and downloaded. In Ghana, way back in the last
century, our school preacher preached a fiery
sermon where the phrase "Gorgeous Gomorrah" was
repeated several times. I asked him how he had
thought that one up. He was Ghanaian, so I couldn't
see him blush as he admitted it came out of a book
of prewritten sermons.

Here are five people. How do they come over to you?
Which are reading and which are talking? What do
you think?

And which are you going to use as a role model?

Practising in front of a mirror itself is worth a check. It can easily lead to self-consciousness. People don't want to see you: they want to see through you – to the God the Holy Trinity.

If you don't think about it, your hands sort of work themselves. You really don't need a mirror. Somehow it's all a bit adolescent.

Read the sermon through by all means and edit it by all means. That makes a lot of sense. But don't beat it into pulp! It needs to have risk, to have spontaneity.

When I was a Curate, I worked with a fellow Curate who did not like me. One day he was off on an important conference and he asked me to preach his Sunday Sermon for him.

I agreed.

So his next comment was "But I shall have to read your sermon first."

I agreed to that too.

His final remark before departure was this: "Make sure that you stick to the text, you have a nasty habit of saying things which are not in what you have written."

After many years of sitting in the pew, I still think he was wrong. The Holy Spirit is there and you really do get inspiration as you preach.

What do you think?

And which picture are you going to use as a role model?

PEOPLE LIKE TO HEAR ABOUT OTHER PEOPLE.

We like to associate ideas with people.

I know a man who works in advertising. He managed to get Ronaldo to endorse his product. Generously, he took his nephew, aged 11, along to the shoot. During the break, instead of going outside for a breather, Ronaldo took time to chat to the nephew, and to give him an autograph. Footballers like that are quite justly revered.

How do you feel after reading that example of a real gentleman? Can you think of any such Christians?

Here are some icebergs to avoid if you can:

Lavrenti Beria, who took over the Great Purge of the 1930s and who remained in charge of the NKVD until the death of Stalin, was very good with children. Svetlana Stalin, daughter of Russia's Dictator, used to sit on his knee and he would read to her with his delicate little spectacles perched right at the top of his nose.

How do you feel after reading that example of Beria, a seriously nasty man? Be very careful who you choose for your example. If, say, you give your favourite politician as an example, then a lot of people will be put off while others will assume that you are from that particular party.

Be careful who you choose as a role model.

President Trump is a superb example of this. Some people like to bash him and to make jokes about his lying. According to some, if President Trump were the Captain of the Titanic, he would deny that there are any icebergs in the North Atlantic and if there were, then it would the penguins who had done it.

If you make remarks like that, you will put off all the people who are fair minded enough to see that you don't get elected POTUS if you are a charmless idiot.

Let us go up a gear.

The church that weds the spirit of the age, ends up a widow in the next.

It was easy to support the British Empire a hundred years ago. Everyone did it. And, of course, it was also obvious that the Church of England was for English people really. If other people, like West Indians, wanted their own church, that was OK. But they had to do it in the West Indies.

That was something which everyone knew to be right.

Today it is laughable.

36/86

Which is why our village church is always closed.

Here is another danger which applies especially to people who are theology geeks:

Islamic Aqeedah is very clear and detailed thing in Quran and Ahadith. There was no difference in Aqeedah among Sahaba Great Salafus Salehin Imams of Ahle Sunnat Wal Jamaat.

How many sermons have I sat through where people were mentioned who I had never heard of (as in the last quotation)? Or clever little Greek, Hebrew and Latin words are thrown in? Theological words rolling along like massive articulated lorries. Or jargon? Why do they do this? Is it to show the Preacher's great knowledge? Nothing turns me off quicker than that. So avoid dropping theologians' names in without introducing them – Bultmann, Professor Lampe, St Augustine, St Ignatius Loyola, St Charles Borromeo, Martin Luther King. Build them in! Tell about their love of God! Their temptations and whether or not they overcame them! The good they did!

Giving an example is such a good idea in sermons. St Paul, Jesus, St Augustine (a very troubled sex life there!), Martha and Mary, are all from the Christian stable. But there are, of course, a lot of influential people outside the Christian Church who can be held up as role models. Jesus himself used to mix freely with tax collectors and Samaritans.

Ron was a down and out I knew in Bedford when I was a Curate there. He stank. His clothes were filthy. He never had any money and was always on the scrounge for fag ends which he picked up from the pavement. One day, as I walked along outside the church, a clean-cut man in a new grey suit walked towards me and said hello. For a moment I could not place him. Then it dawned: Ron! He told me he had become a Christian and that had turned his life round. Then with a cheerful smile, he walked on.

Inspirational people need not be famous.

Summary:

If you want to illustrate a point, or to add flavour to the sermon, pick some people! Or just one person. Tell us about why they fit the case you are presenting! Hold them up as an example.

AUTHORITY.

By what authority do you do this?

> Mark 11.27 After their return to Jerusalem, Jesus was walking in the temple courts, and the chief priests, scribes, and elders came up to Him. 28 "By what authority are You doing these things?" they asked. "And who gave You the authority to do them?" 29 "I will ask you one question," Jesus replied, "and if you answer Me, I will tell you by what authority I am doing these things....

By what authority...

For us Catholics, Authority rests with the Church. The Church produced the Bible. The Church (Catechism, Canon Law) says what is good and what is bad. The Church (General Council) decides what is Christian and what is not. And it changes over the years.

Ask any devout Catholic, who can remember what it was like before the 1960s, about the changes which Vatican II brought on...

For Protestants, the Bible itself is the traditional authority. That and the Holy Spirit which inspires the chosen people with the flame of Pentecost. Then there is each individual

40/86

Protestant church which usually depends on some kind of a majority vote.

Protestants have an impressive list of determined people.

- Horatio Nelson,

- Jane Austen,

- the Wesleys,

- Mr Gladstone,

- Otto von Bismarck,

- Winston Churchill,

- Her Majesty the Queen...

- Thomas Clarkson, the Quakers and William Wilberforce who between them abolished slavery.

- Martin Luther who faced being burned alive for his protests.

Back to the Bible: Quoting the Bible can work very well in Church among Church people. That, after all, is what we believe. But we do have to remember that it does not work outside the church building.

What is more there are some unpopular bits.

41/86

I cannot see a woman bishop or a woman priest choosing this as her text:

> As in all the congregations of the Lord's people. Women should remain silent in the churches, they are not allowed to speak, but must be in submission, as the law says. If they want to inquire about something, they should ask their own husbands at home; for it is disgraceful for a woman to speak in the church."[1Cor. 14:33-35]

> A woman must quietly receive instruction with entire submissiveness. But I do not allow a woman to teach or exercise authority over a man, but to remain quiet. For it was Adam who was first created, and then Eve. And it was not Adam who was deceived, but the woman being deceived, fell into transgression. But women will be preserved through the bearing of children if they continue in faith and love and sanctity with self-restraint. [1Tim. 2:9–15]

Also, of course, Paul believed that women should veil themselves on almost Islamic lines.

But I want you to realize that the head of every man is Christ, and the head of the woman is man, and the head of Christ is God. Every man who prays or prophesies with his head covered dishonours his head. But every woman who prays or prophesies with her head uncovered dishonours her head—it is the same as having her head shaved. For if a woman does not cover her head, she might as well have her hair cut off; but if it is a disgrace for a woman to have her hair cut off or her head shaved, then she should cover her head. A man ought not to cover his head, since he is the image and glory of God; but woman is the glory of man. For man did not come from woman, but woman from man; neither was man created for woman, but woman for man. [1Cor 11:3–9]

Paul also supported slavery.

Were you a slave when you were called? Don't let it trouble you – although if you can gain your freedom, do so. (1 Corinthians 7:21, NIV)

Slaves, obey your earthly masters with respect and fear, and with sincerity of heart, just as you would obey Christ. (Ephesians 6:5, NIV)

Slave traders? Just as bad as gay people:

> ... for adulterers and perverts, for slave traders and liars and perjurers. (1 Timothy 1:10 NIV)

Can you imagine a gay bishop or priest reading these texts out:

> Or do you not know that the unrighteous will not inherit the kingdom of God? Do not be deceived: neither the sexually immoral, nor idolaters, nor adulterers, nor men who practice homosexuality, nor thieves, nor the greedy, nor drunkards, nor revilers, nor swindlers will inherit the kingdom of God. And such were some of you. But you were washed, you were sanctified, you were justified in the name of the Lord Jesus Christ and by the Spirit of our God. (1 Corinthians 6:9-11)

> For this reason, God gave them up to dishonourable passions. For their women exchanged natural relations for those that are contrary to nature; and the men likewise gave up natural relations with women and were consumed with passion for one another, men committing shameless acts with men and receiving in themselves the due penalty for their

error. And since they did not see fit to acknowledge God, God gave them up to a debased mind to do what ought not to be done. (Romans 1:26-28)

Just as Sodom and Gomorrah and the surrounding cities, which likewise indulged in sexual immorality and pursued unnatural desire, serve as an example by undergoing a punishment of eternal fire. (Jude 1:7)

And all this is balanced by the often quoted Galatians passage:

There is neither Jew nor Greek,

slave nor free,

male nor female,

for you are all one in Christ Jesus.

(Galatians 3:28 NIV)

Maybe you can explain?

Just taking the Bible as the literal Word of God will not convince anyone outside the church. The Bible stretches right across history and it reflects the times in which it was written.

The Qur'an was, it is believed by Muslims, dictated to the Messenger of God by the Angel Gabriel word for word. To question just one word is, therefore, to question God Himself and that is a terrible blasphemy.

The Bible – all of it – is not like that. It is written by inspired human beings, fallible children of their time.

And it certainly inspires us today too – or it does me. And it is, among other things, usually a very good read.

But just using it is a sledge hammer is not, I am afraid, possible. It has to be treated like a gentle suggestion.

Think of it this way. If someone says to you that to go to heaven, you must not eat or drink anything all day in the month of Ramadan because it says so in the Qur'an, would you believe them? Not unless you were a Muslim. I am afraid that today the Bible is a closed book to most people in Europe. It is not a dog whistle any more.

A Protestant Minister was preaching a hellfire sermon in Northern Ireland. After reading out several fiery texts about hell and damnation from the Holy Book, he proclaimed: "And there shall be weeping and gnashing of teeth!!!"

An old lady in the front row moved her toothless gums in protest. "But I haven't got any teeth."

"TEETH," shouted the preacher, "WILL BE PROVIDED!!!"

I am not sure why I put that one in.

Summary: By what authority do you talk to people for ten minutes or so without them interrupting?

All organisations love jargon, and the Christian Church is as bad at this as any. We can sum up the most important ideas in one word. Here are a few examples:

Crucifixion, Atonement, Resurrection, Easter, Paraclete, Mary, Jesus...

Centuries ago, we thought we understood exactly what these words all meant. So we assume today that everyone knows.

They do not.

- *Christmas* is when the sleigh bells ring out and Father Christmas comes for the kiddies, who know the

names of every single one of the reindeer, where
Santa lives, what he looks like and why he is nice.

People who say that our Christian faith is stupid should
remember that there aren't many sleighs in Reigate and as for
young children sitting on a strange old man's lap! Where is
the Safeguarding there? Aged six, I used to wonder how one
single man could go down the chimneys of every single house
in the world at the same time – midnight on Christmas Eve. I
didn't see how it was sensible somehow.

- *Easter* is when the holiday season begins. The Easter
  Bunny has become more popular, but of course there
  are always Easter Eggs...

We Christians have to stand up and put our case. Christmas is
the miraculous time when God (The Father, the First Cause,
the Creator of the universe - not just a galaxy or two,) came to
earth and became human (incarnation, kenosis, Messiah). In
real time.

Easter is when God's Son died on the cross after three show
trials and a severe beating. (Cross? Oh yes, crosses make nice
gold earrings. "Has it got a little man on it?")

Then what? He was there again, talking, being recognised, cooking, eating!

The stories beat anything, yes anything, in literature by a long way. Matter of fact. Simple. Common sense even. Outrageous too. And quite unlike any of the competition - Roman, Greek, Jewish or Muslim.

It is our task to get that message across. Pick out one of our jargon words and just explain it as carefully and clearly as the writers of the Gospels did. Modern scholarship will, at last, support you. The days of Richard Dawkins are now past.

Richard Dawkins, that handsome charming man, presented our faith as if it were a hellfire sermon! He did not understand that the survival of the fittest and evolution neatly answer the question "How did God create the world". In no way do they answer the question "Who created the world?" And his god is a god of hatred, of severe punishment, not the God who cares passionately about his creation at all.

Oh – and forget the children. You should speak to your congregation as if you were explaining the internet, or your latest holiday to your father or mother. If you must include the children – do it separately. They may be the church of the future, but without their parents pushing them they won't be there next week.

Summary: Keep it simple and reach into the hearts of your listeners.

You have got to look as if you know what you are talking about.

For instance, in the discussion of whether or not cannabis should be legalised:

> "We've just witnessed a historic vote for Canada, the end of 90 years of prohibition," said Tony Dean, the senator who sponsored the bill in the chamber. "Now we can start to tackle some of the harms of cannabis. We can start to be proactive in public education. We'll see the end of criminalization and we can start addressing Canada's $7 billion illegal market."

90 years. $7 billion dollar market. So those two facts go to prove that accepting cannabis use must be right for everyone. It looks as if he knows the facts. It is conclusive.

Dropping figures into your sermon will be unusual and the figures will make people sit up and listen. Stats spice it up and make it familiar. And that goes for dates too. Luke and Matthew, to take just two examples, give specific dates for the events in their Gospels. We must not be afraid follow their example.

And today, in the age of the internet, research is so easy to do. I know nothing about this subject of cannabis legalisation, but the quotation above gives the (totally false) impression that I am bang up to date.

Details, of course, make your sermon interesting.

A man said. - boring.

On the afternoon of 27th July 1987, a tall African was talking to a friend outside a shop in central Liverpool... – you want to hear more about it.

Unpack the Saints! Unpack the Apostles! Unpack the times they lived in!

If you are speaking about a moral question in your sermon – abortion, divorce, marriage, giving to charity, safeguarding – it is much more convincing if you centre on the facts – or some carefully selected facts. Be like Senator Tony Dean in Canada.

This leads on to a bigger question.

We have to be very careful here. If we come to tribal conclusions, then we have to realise that they are just for us in the tribe. They are not necessarily universal moral truths.

- "The Church has always said..." (Which Church?)

- "The Bible teaches..." (Where exactly?)

- "Christians believe..." (Ahem!)

Quote the Bible by all means – that is what Church is for. But although the Bible rings out in Church, that is not the case in the street outside. You might as well be quoting - I don't know – from *Das Kapital*. We have to use common currency if we are going to take our faith outside the church doors. Dirhams do not work in Doncaster. Pounds do not work in Peru.

Feelings are personal. Let's give an example: some people feel very strongly that homosexuality is wrong and that the Lord hates it. But that is not going to convince people outside the church doors – or even inside them – to change their behaviour. Conscience is an excellent guide to personal behaviour: it fails when it becomes tribal. Everyone does their own thing. We all have feelings. Why are mine better than yours?

And Human Rights? "I know my rights". Yes, but who is going to give those rights to you? And what if other people have Human Rights as well? There is no Right to Life in many countries in Africa or the Middle East today. Appealing to

Rights often shows that you have no intention of listening:
you are shutting down the argument.

Outside the Church, morality is a pretty dodgy subject.

We need to point this out.

Summary: To be convincing, we must know both sides in
some detail, but more important, we must know what the
Will of God is, we must know the pathway (however difficult it
may be), and we must trust that God Himself supports us.

When we get that right, we are invincible.

Bible References, Research.

This is a picture of Tom Holland who used a lot of historical research for his outstanding work on Islam, "In the Shadow of the Sword." Because of his imaginative investigation into the birth of Islam, his book is fascinating, exciting and totally convincing too. Without the details, it would have been terminally boring. In fact, it is so successful that he is getting death threats!

Christianity is a Faith which is historical. We believe that Jesus is a real man who came to earth in the early years of the Roman Empire, a man who really went around a certain place on earth, teaching, joking, laughing, weeping, healing and appreciating. He was tortured and executed by the Romans in public. He then reappeared to the consternation of his companions until he was taken up into heaven.

All this is as historical as, say, Napoleon, the Korean war or The Russian Revolution.

So we can treat it like any other historical event centred round a historical person.

What is the archaeological evidence for the crucifixion? Who did the digging? Who did the report? What did they say? Some of the historical characters in the story are fascinating. Herod killed three of his sons – I think, without looking up the details. Pilate had a fascinating history too – always in trouble with the Emperor. St Peter is presented as a rough, rather impulsive fisherman in the Gospels, so how did he manage to write those highly polished letters?

This could well lead on to research into the documentation which has been so carefully handed down – ink made out of a growth on oak trees, pens either made out of metal or else goose feathers, written by an expert on a special table on vellum (what is that?) or, perhaps, paper (where did that come from? Unveil a very strange history for the introduction of paper into Europe!).

Also look at the mistakes! They are fascinating as well. For example, when Jesus is handed some sour wine on the cross, it is extended on a "hyssopo". Hyssop is a tiny little plant which could never be used in this way. But there it is in the text. Now what? Well, some sensible copyist made it make sense: "hysso" - a "spear" which, of course, makes much more sense. So we have two readings. The rule is that you accept the more difficult one. Now what? Which is right?

We need not be afraid of our history. And it can be fascinating too.

Figures are helpful. And they are so easy to get hold of nowadays. Simply Google *how many christians have been affected by the syrian war* (note the lazy punctuation!) and this is what comes up:

> Syrian Christians, in line with their fellow citizens, have been badly affected by the Syrian Civil War. According to Syrian law, all Syrian men of adult age with brothers are eligible for military conscription, including Christians. Since the outbreak of the Syrian Civil War in 2011, 300,000 to 900,000 Christians have left the country, but as the situation began to stabilize in 2017 following recent army gains, return of

electricity and water to many areas and stability returning to many going back...

As the Islamic State, insurgents, and government forces battle in Syria, the population of Christians there continues to decline, from 1,250,000 in 2011 to less than 500,000 this year, according to ADF International, which advocates for religious freedom worldwide.

That took me just a couple of minutes to download. I haven't bothered to unpack it. And it brings home the full horror of the tyranny that the British ophthalmologist, Bashar al Assad, has brought on our fellow believers.

We have to be very careful when we fill our sermon with figures though. They are like alcohol: a little is lovely and very stimulating. Too much sends people to sleep. (PS The same goes for "generous portions of scripture" too!)

But you knew that already.

GRAB THE FUTURE!

If you look at the state of our village churches, the future is the enemy. Only old people go there when the church is reluctantly unlocked for the hour for Sunday Worship. The Prayer Book went ages ago along with the vicarage, the vicar and the church hall. So did the Holy Communion quite often, to be replaced by a "joyous service for the whole family". We don't need the crystal ball to see that in a few years, the buildings themselves will have fallen into disrepair and then become ruins. I remember someone writing in white paint on a parish church – GOD IS DEAD. That was way back in the last century. Today nearly every church and chapel in the land proclaims that the person who wrote that was right.

Obviously, time is the enemy for us churchgoers!

Let's just take a look at all this.

The Church of England is the national church. That means that the supreme Governor is Her Majesty the Queen. Regimental flags, often covered in mould, hang like spiders' webs from the walls. War memorials adorn the windows. Books of Remembrance of the Fallen (1914-1918) stand in their glass topped wooden lecterns. The Church of England stretches round the world in all the places where the British Empire once bought peace and prosperity.

Now, of course, the Empire is no more. Her Majesty the Queen presides over a very dysfunctional family and there are murmurs about the future of the monarchy. There is a feeling of renewal, of trashing the past. Of treating our noble history as something disreputable. "Do I smell racism and exploitation?" asks the comment on the web.

But the Christian Faith is way beyond that short time scale.

I have just painted a picture of Abraham's slave girl, Hagar. Abraham (aged 99!) was married to an old lady (Sarah) and the couple had no children. Abraham was given a ridiculous promise. His children would be as numerous as the stars in the sky! God Almighty promised him personally, "I will make you exceedingly fruitful: I will make nations out of you, and kings shall spring from you... As for your wife Sarah, she shall be the mother of nations: the kings of many people will spring from her."

This to Abraham who was childless!

Even when, in desperation, Abraham took his slave girl, Hagar, and had a boy (Ishmael) with her, Sarah, his wife, got so jealous that Hagar was driven out into the desert to die along with her son.

Then, by a miracle, Sarah did actually become pregnant and give birth to one boy – Isaac. At which point God told Abraham to sacrifice Isaac!

So that meant Ishmael was right out of the picture and Isaac was not going to inherit. Was God's promise just a cruel hoax?

Of course, today, the promise has been fulfilled – after three millennia. Hagar is the mother of a billion Muslims, kings and all, and in the Ka'aba at Mecca, so they say, stands the very well from which she drank and which saved her life. Muslims take home the sacred water and store it in their homes. The Well of Zamzam.

Isaac is one of the Jewish patriarchs. There are a lot of his descendants today in the world, despite the best efforts of several governments.

Christians, too, are included in the children of Abraham. That makes even more billions of people.

My point?

Time, to God, is not the same as time to us humans. So we must not judge from what is happening at the moment. We work on a much larger canvas.

And we also look *forward*, unlike a lot of dreamers in the media, the television and the social media who are living for today, worrying about today's troubles, today's vulnerable, today's gadfly people.

"Thy Kingdom come (*future*), thy will be done on earth as it is in heaven."

So let's use *future* words in our sermons. Words like *new, young, visionary, progressive, up to date, youth, modern* are good words to use.

God is working His purpose out, as year succeeds on year. Now is the time to act, don't just sit there all miserable. Thy kingdom come...

Summary: We are the future. God is there in the beginning, He is here now, and He always will be.

HOW WOULD YOU LIKE IT IF SOMEONE DID THAT TO YOU? THERE ARE VICTIMS HERE...

Victimhood is one of the most powerful arguments there is. It is an appeal for help. The damsel in distress syndrome.

On our local Nextdoor site, a lady wrote, at the height of the Corona Virus lock-down, "My heart is breaking." She then went on to explain how her neighbour had suffered a series of calamities, some small, some more serious, which was destroying her family. In the end it all came down to an appeal for money. And it flowed in! It really did. The words "My heart is breaking" went straight to the hearts of the community. Nobody likes to see a lady with a broken heart.

In the past, the crucifixion was used a lot in this way. It was very easy for preachers to describe, in ferocious detail, the sufferings of Jesus on the cross. The (excellent) film of "The

Passion of the Christ" by Mel Gibson did the same thing. You really felt sorry for Jesus. For Catholics, the Stations of the Cross and the reading of the Passion do the same thing. As did "Jesus Christ Superstar". Jesus the victim.

In the Catholic Church, we also have Cafod which regularly starts the appeal off with a victim – usually an African child – who has to walk miles for water, then carry the bucket home on her head before trudging the five miles to her school which, unfortunately, has no books, just a blackboard and chalk and a semi-trained teacher. A victim, like Jesus.

South Park has the little, thin African called Starvin' Marvin.

It works very well for Christians who are being martyred for the cause. Syria is a good example where the oldest church in the world – one still speaking in Jesus' Aramaic – is systematically being wiped out. One Sunday this was brought home very starkly by our priest, who travelled a lot in the Middle East, saying that the incense at Mass came from Syria and had been a present from a Syrian Christian.

Some Muslims have adopted the idea too. The suicide murderers who deliberately kill fellow humans, in the name of God, and in direct disobedience to the Koran, call themselves "Ashuhada'" - martyrs. Rabbi Jonathan Sacks, himself a graduate of Cambridge University where he read philosophy before becoming Chief Rabbi, weighs into them in his powerful book "Not in God's Name". He explains carefully how victims have to be deliberately made – by enemies. And it is therefore right, once you are a victim, to point the finger and demand recompense. Victims and violence go hand in hand, he says.

For Christians, this victimhood used to be done by, for example, Fox's Book of Martyrs, with illustrations of people being tortured to death. Protestant martyrs – Catholic torturers. The Spanish Inquisition... But Catholics can be victims too - in Ireland Catholics are familiar with the struggle for independence and their victimhood at the hands of King William and, even today, Oliver Cromwell. In Liverpool, Hillsborough demands justice from the victims' families.

Jews, with very good reason, remember the holocaust, which was one of the causes of the modern state of Israel. It comes as no surprise that mass murder of totally innocent people produces a real hatred of the wicked Nazis who did it. Victims demanding justice and, in this case, getting it.

The Palestinians claim victimhood against the Israelis too.

Used appropriately, victimhood can unite a group and bring a sense of importance and urgency for justice. It is a very powerful tool for the preacher of the Word. But victimhood is an extremely dangerous one as well. So use it, but only after a lot of prayerful meditation.

Summary: Victims and Violence begin with the same letter.

LIST THE ADVANTAGES.

Sales people are very good at this. It is called listing the advantages.

Sales people have to learn their script. It is detailed. It describes the product with affection. Only the good points are listed: bad points come later. (If at all!)

Next time you buy something, listen to the sales rep. They will go through the advantages with great care!

Learn from them and do the same when you, too, come to make your argument.

Lovingly talk about the advantages one by one.

It works very well in a sermon too.

Talk about the glory of God. (Hint: the end of the Book of Job.)

Man, after all, is a tiny little virus on a minute little planet. The sun is the centre of our galaxy and the planets are little specks that circle round it. We have our little moon.

Further off – and we are here talking about millions of light years – are other galaxies. And then what? Nobody has any idea.

67/86

We can guess, of course. But nobody really knows.

God, on the other hand, does know.

He runs the creation, enormous as it is. He also runs the atoms and the electrons and the elements which he uses to make them too.

He plans the whole thing out, runs the whole thing on regular scientific principles which man can understand up to a point.

And God cares passionately about us – us - the tiny little speck on another tiny little speck - the planet we live on.

It is a Magnificat moment. Why did He choose us, for heaven's sake?

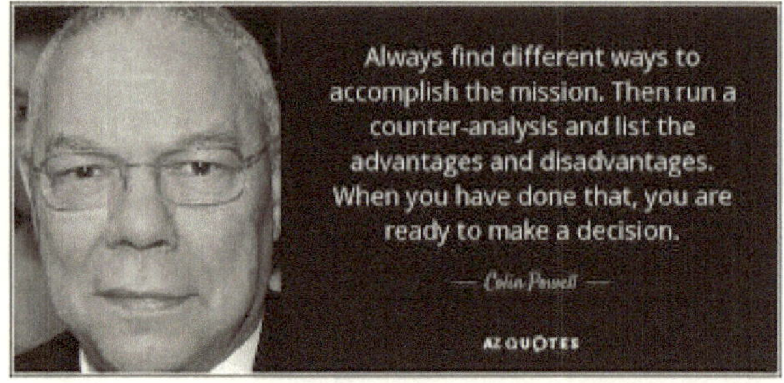

Do you weigh it up by drawing up a list of disadvantages too?

Well that is up to you. If you are talking to people who appreciate seeing both sides of the story, then, of course, you must do that. If, on the other hand, you are trying to sell an idea, then don't. It depends if you are trying to praise God and His Creation or if you are arguing a point. Poetry or prose?

Summary: As soon as you list the advantages, the whole thing comes to life and it is surprisingly easy to do. Especially if you are talking about one of your favourite passages in the Bible. (My own favourites are the books of Proverbs and Ecclesiastes.)

DEDUCTION

We start with something obvious, something that everyone can agree with. Then we draw down a conclusion from that.

Let's take an easy example : Human life is sacred. What can we deduce from that though?

Do we go on to talk about abortion? (Yawn) or perhaps some war or other?

In a Catholic Church in the North of England at the time of the Iraq invasion in 2003, a young man (well he thought he was young anyway) perched on the chancel steps with a guitar singing "Not in my name." We sat through it. At the end of the service an elderly lady and I discussed the song. We both agreed that if the Prime Minister called for a war effort, then we ought, as loyal citizens, to go along with his decision. This was never mentioned by the young man. He assumed that he was simply telling the one and only truth: human life is precious.

The invasion turned out to be a disaster, and the British were roundly humiliated in Basra. But she still had a point. She was putting loyalty to her country above loyalty to a general principle.

There are always two sides to a deduction. We have to respect both sides. Even in the most obvious cases there is an opposition.

In fact, the elderly lady and I were agreed that human life is not always so sacred that nothing can be allowed to risk it.

A good example is Charity Giving. Churches are very good indeed at charity giving. And there are countless cases in the Bible in both Old and New Testaments of generous giving. When Elijah is hiding from wicked King Ahab, he sees an old widow collecting sticks. He calls for a drink of water and some bread. She tells him that she is collecting a couple of sticks for a fire to make some cakes out of the very last of her flour and oil. Then she is going to lie down with her son and die.

Elijah asks her to give him that very flour and oil for himself in a cake! He tells her that the flour and oil will last her until she can get some more. She generously believes him.

Obediently she listens, goes inside and, as the prophet has foretold, the oil and flour do not fail until the Lord sends rain on the land.

But she didn't know that when she was so generous. She was prepared to give the very last bit of her flour and her son's food to a stranger and to be generous enough to trust his word.

Generosity! The woman who anointed Jesus with expensive oil of spikenard was generous too. It must have been one of her most precious and personal cosmetics - her hair conditioner, her Chanel. Saved, no doubt, for very special occasions. But she took it out and used it on someone else.

But generosity is not stupidity.

How much of the Charity money goes to the CEO and his/her officials? How much goes to the local dictator to be spent on armaments? How much of the money is spent on people in the administration working their computers in front of a nice cuppa?

How little of the charity money dribbles through to the people who are in desperate need? The sick old man? The blind child?

I must have sat through so many little talks about charity and very rarely if ever have I heard any mention of this.

Deduction must include the objections. Otherwise it becomes a rant.

And the New Testament is so full of Rules that can be used for deduction!

The Ten Commandments are one such set of rules. Then there are the Beatitudes. Of course, there is the golden rule which spreads across many other religions too – Do not do anything to anyone else which you would not like to be done to yourself. Do as you would be done by. Love your neighbour as yourself. And "You shall love the Lord your God with all your heart, with all your Soul and with all your Strength".

What does that mean to me in the pew?

Summary: There is so much input here for a sermon. There are so many things that everyone believes.

WHAT IF?

The trouble with Judaism, the trouble with Islam, the trouble with Christianity and the trouble with most (not all) religions is that they are very, very old. We've heard it all before. The threadbare stories are repeated year after year and it is very hard to get them fresh. So people stop listening. Most of us stopped during our adolescence. And these ideas and stories remain part of childhood – nice but babyish.

Christmas? The nativity play – out with the tea towels! Cute little girl carrying a dolly and some wretched child dressed in his dressing gown with another tea towel on his head for

Joseph.

Easter? Easter egg hunt in a desperate attempt to rejuvenate the ancient ceremony of Eostra when the Green Man comes,

73/86

breathing out fresh shoots from his open mouth (In Botticelli's picture of spring, the green man is the woman on the right) and everyone goes on holiday to the Med – or beyond. And don't forget the Eostra idol – the gormless Easter Bunny.

In fact, the Bible stories are so familiar that they are largely neglected.

What if we actually read them instead of going through the usual rituals?

What if they had never happened in the first place? What if God's son had never come to earth and been executed and then reappeared? What would life be like then?

In Australia a brilliant artist won the prize for the best picture. I forget just what it was. He painted chunky portraits which were lively and arresting. After a few years of success, he turned to drink and drugs. His paintings turned into slop draining down the canvas. One night, in a stupor, he went to sleep lying on his right arm. When he woke up it was paralysed. His friends left him. He eventually died, very young, having achieved nothing – except self indulgence.

What a waste! But without any form of belief holding him together, why not? There are many such celebrities. Just open the paper and read about them. Without any form of hope, that is what happens. Why not?

What if Martin Luther had not started off the Reformation?

74/86

We would still be going to stand at Mass where the Priest would do it all himself in Latin (which nobody understands), he would then elevate the sacred host and probably consume it alone. In the darkened church, with the dimly coloured light streaming through the stained glass, the incense wafting upwards, perhaps some plainsong or chanting, the mystery would end in a blessing – in Latin. Then people would leave, being careful to sprinkle (or take) some holy water to ward off diseases and the ever present demons. In the picture, notice Jesus dancing on the altar ready to enter the sacred bread. What kind of religion is that?

I once attended the Russian Orthodox Funeral of a friend of mine. One hour of singing in Russian. Lots of incense. Very impressive – for the first twenty minutes. Then mystified boredom creeps in, resisted at first then reluctantly accepted. You leave grateful but deadened. Your mind has not been fed.

And we would probably be still in the middle ages if Martin Luther had not been brave enough to display his feelings in public.

And today? No cars, no modern medicine. Lots of early death. Childbirth often a death sentence. The sky? A blue bowl with God's Word spoken to astrologers and magicians through the position of the planets. We would be hungry, a bit drunk perhaps, bereaved almost certainly, cold, dirty, sick...

And of course, the end of your sermon is easy: you simply say what happened and how grateful we ought to be! Remember the ten lepers who were cured by Jesus. Just one of them actually came back to say thank you. We need to be that one.

Here are some ideas:

- What if the Church of England was simply closed down tomorrow? (What if the Covid 19 Church lock-down had never ended?)

- What if Jesus really did perform all those miracles?

- What if Islam took over our country?

- What if Jesus really did come back from the dead?

- What if the Holy Spirit simply did not exist?

- What if there were no clergy at all?

- What if nobody got married?

- What if God did not exist and Richard Dawkins was right?

- Imagine there's no Heaven. It's easy if you try... (Yup – St John Lennon who was martyred for the cause of – what exactly?)

Summary: What if? is a very helpful stimulus for a sermon.

	URGENT	NOT URGENT
IMPORTANT	Quadrant I *urgent and* *important* **DO**	Quadrant II *not urgent* *but important* **PLAN**
NOT IMPORTANT	Quadrant III *urgent but* *not important* **DELEGATE**	Quadrant IV *not urgent and* *not important* **ELIMINATE**

I think there are three separate things going on here. The first is...This is a very complicated subject. Let's just break it up into its seventeen separate parts shall we. First...

Theology, let us face it, is a scientific discipline. If we simply bumble on without thinking, then sooner or later we will start to think silly things are true. Some people, for example, think that disease is spread through putrid air. If not enough people live in a city, they stop disturbing the air and it settles down and becomes putrid. In Gades, near modern Gibraltar, people believed that a man had found a pot with a lead seal. Carelessly he broke the seal and a puff of smoke came out. That smoke was the spell which bound the plague into the bottle! After that, Gades became a very marshy, unpleasant place to live in.

Religion and superstition are two sides of the same coin...

I know a young Mum who thinks that at the end of her road live some djinns – evil spirits who inhabit the trees and bushes. She says a sentence out of the Koran every time she passes to ward them off.

Let's break things down into separate parts to understand it.

This works very well for theology.

Let's take an example to show what this means. In his book on *Jesus of Nazareth*, Pope Benedict discusses the cleansing of the temple. Why did Jesus do it?

1. First of all, there is the question of whether or not he was a revolutionary, a Zealot. Was he doing it to show his left wing credentials, fighting against authority? His disgust at capitalism? His attack on the priestly income where they took a cut on the animals who were bought for sacrifice?

2. Secondly, was it because, as he said, God's house was not meant to be a den of thieves. It was a house of prayer. Selling and swindling were not fitting in such a holy place. (Does this affect *Flog it* being held in a cathedral? Or a bouncy castle in another cathedral perhaps?)

3. Thirdly, there is another possibility. Zeal for the Lord is a sign of the Messiah. Jesus was showing that he was the promised Messiah in accordance with the Old Testament. He was being truly zealous. Zeal - "for your house has consumed me..."

By giving all three alternatives, Pope Benedict gives us a real insight into why Jesus cleansed the temple. Without that we might just assume that one of the three reasons was the right one. And that could lead to dangerous action.

If we want to describe anything, it is a good idea to break it down into different parts.

- The Christian life starts with baptism, it continues through the Eucharist and finishes up in heaven.

- There are, of course, seven sacraments.

- There are four Gospels.

- There were twelve disciples. (13 counting Judas.)

Jesus' ministry falls into several stages, depending on how you divide it. More complicated is the life of St Paul. St Paul had several (Is it really just three?) missionary journeys. How does the Council of Jerusalem fit in? St Paul's life fell into two parts – before the Damascus Road conversion and after it. How do the parts compare with each other? How did he end his life? What is the evidence?

There are three monotheistic religions: Judaism, Islam and Christianity. How do they compare with each other? What do they all have in common? How do they differ? Does it matter today? If we neglect to talk about the three religions, then there is a danger that terrible ignorance creeps in. I can give several examples of very influential and clever people who know nothing about Islam and "Zionism" and yet who hold very definite views on what needs to be done about them! Why are the Christian Churches so loath to talk about things like that in the weekly services?

And so on.

Dividing things up into their separate parts also works for moral questions.

There are different ways to confront the issue of divorce. Should divorced people receive the blessed sacrament?

1. First we can take the simple Gospel view that divorce is simply wrong. We can easily find the places in the New Testament where divorce is condemned except under extreme provocation by googling Wikipedia. And then we can compare them precisely. Huck or a Concordance for the geeks! When, where is he when he gives his views? What exactly does he say? Who is there at the time? How does it compare with the Jewish Law? Why is it important 2000 years later?

2. Secondly we can see from our own lives that divorce is sometimes necessary. Being married, for example, to a very cruel person is not good for anyone, let alone the children. Examples from real life (without names!) are always interesting so long as nobody - nobody – knows who you are talking about! And there is always *Wuthering Heights* to fall back on.

3. Thirdly we can ask what marriage really is and use the Bible to show what Jesus presents to us as the ideal. What do you think? Tell us!

If that doesn't appeal, then God is the Holy Trinity – Father, Son and Holy Spirit. How does that work then?

Summary: Dividing difficult topics into parts is helpful. And it is very rarely done too. Surprise the congregation!

TELL ME THE OLD, OLD STORY.
Judging by the notices on our Anglican Parish Church, there
are constant attempts to make the church relevant today.

The children are the Church of the future! So the big service is,
of course, Mothering Sunday where you can bring the
children. Five OAPs turned out for it in our village church.
Then there is the Grand Easter Egg Hunt which took place at
the Mother Church of the Group. I have no idea what
happened there. Christmas had a Midnight Mass. Hallowe'en
was not celebrated - which surprised me. Two services of Holy
Communion a month in a cosy little nook under the arches
with heating and comfy chairs. The altar frontal is always the
same one and in the corner are some little games and toys for
the children. The toys are always in the same place,
untouched.

The numbers for Holy Communion in the Services Register? In
no case did they come into double figures.

If you do not preach the Gospel and deliver the sacraments
properly and with explanation and love, then that is what
happens.

So we do not need to be clever. It is all there waiting to be
delivered, renewed and exciting. *Semper reformanda* – always
ready for change. We need to find out how we can get
through to ordinary people with our message of hope. Man is
not a fluke. Our planet may be small, but God loves it enough
to sacrifice his Son for us. He loves us enough to make sure

that he gets his harvest of faithful people who return His love
too

If little, then large: would this man destroy his train, however annoying it was being?